Good, Better, Best!

By PM Ogilvie

Copyright © 2014 ProRisk Ent. Ltd.
Box 253, Alberta Beach, Alberta, Canada T0E 0A0

All rights reserved.

ISBN-13: **978-0978052041**
ISBN-10: **0978052048**

(ProRisk Ent. Ltd.)

The content of this book is for general educational purposes only and should not be construed as medial advice or child rearing advice. It's For Fun!

DEDICATION

To parents who have toddlers and children who love to play, sing, draw and make friends!

Thank you also to www.graphicstock.com as the subscription-based resource for all the wonderful royalty-free photos.

CONTENTS

Slurping
Skittering
Coloring
Smelly Room
Rah-Rah
Wave Your Flag
Jump to the Sky
Kick a Ball
Happy Birthday
Going on a Picnic
A Gladder Grin
Wetter Water
Starfish in the Ocean
Ride a Rainbow
Puppies
Sunshine Above the Clouds
Grandpa
Christmas
My Family
Little Brother Sitter
The World is a Love Letter

...his and her BEST!

When my mom buys me ice cream

My tummy feels good.

When she adds a scoop of red,

My tummy feels better.

When the slurp falls on my shirt,

And mom says, "It doesn't matter."

My tummy feels best!

When I wear my squeaky shiny shoes

I ride and feel good

When I wear my cool sneakers

I ride and feel better

When I've nothing on my feet

I skitter so much faster,

I ride and feel best!

When I color the sun pink

My picture looks good

When I color the sun purple

My picture looks better

When I color the sun yellow

And it sparkles and glitters

I love my picture best!

When my room's a little messy

I sniff... it smells good

When mom washes dirty jeans

Sniff... ah the room smells better

When I find that old cheese

Under my bright blue sweater

My room smells best!

When I practice my cheer

The Rah-Rah sounds good

When I practice one time

The Rah-Rah sounds better

When I practice each day

No matter the weather,

The Rah-Rah sounds best!

When I think about my country

My heart feels good

When I hold a flag in my hand

My heart feels better

When I wave it and wave it up in the air

No matter how it flutters,

My heart feels best!

When we jump to the sky

We feel good

When we jump to touch the clouds

We feel so much better

When we jiggle our arms

And legs we do shutter,

The jumping feels best!

When I practice my kick

The Ball rolls good

When I practice side kicks

The Ball spins better

When I practice each day

No matter the red sweater,

The Ball rolls best!

When I sing in the hammock

My voice sounds good

When I swing to and fro

My singing sounds better

When I practice Happy Birthday

No matter how flatter,

The HAAAAAAPPY sounds best!

When our family does a picnic

Momma's salad tastes good

When she adds some salad dressing

The salad tastes better

When she fills my plate

And adds a hotdog on the platter,

The picnic lunch tastes best!

When we ride in our blue car

I feel so good

When we drive down the street

I feel even better

When Poppa drives on the highway

The smile on my face is gladder,

Family outing feels best!

When we boat on the lake

My wet fingers feel good

When Poppa rows out to the middle

My wet fingers feel better

When he splashes and turns

And my whole hand gets wetter,

My love of water feels best!

When we vacation at the ocean

I feel very good

When I wade into the water

I feel so much better

When I imagine what shells live on its floor

The bottom starfish all scattered

I love all those creatures best!

When I think about my friends

I feel good

When we can play all the day

I feel better

When I imagine we slide down a rainbow

Down, down colors so bright together

This rainbow feels the best!

When my family and I travel

Boy I feel good

When we visit a castle

I feel even better

When we take our little puppie

And her little feet go pitter-patter

I love this vacation the best!

When the sun hides behind rainy clouds

I feel good

Because my friend has an umbrella

I feel better

Momma says sun shines above the clouds

And the rain doesn't matter,

So we scrunch under and feel best!

When my grandpa comes to visit

I feel so good

When we go for a walk

I feel better

When he buys us ice cream

And we giggle together,

I love grandpa's visit the best!

When Christmas comes to my house

I feel good

I dream about Santa, presents and stuff

And I feel better

When we bring home a tree

And light the star from a ladder

I love this season the best!

When I'm with my family

I feel good

When we play with balloons

I feel better

When we visit the park

And all day we chatter

I love my family the best!

When momma throws the beach ball

I feel good

When my little brother can catch it

I feel better

Because if he plays with my mom

I don't have to be his baby-sitter,

I feel the best!

When I think about my home

My mind feels good

When I think about my family

My heart feels better

When I spread my arms out

Imagine my world is a love letter

My mind and heart feel the best

Today I learned something new

That best, better and good

Can explain all sorts of things.

And that I never use better

When comparing my friends

Because each one matters,

And fills my heart with his and her best!

ABOUT THE AUTHOR

PM Ogilvie, Certified Coach and former school teacher has a love of children. Her training about energy, belief systems and cool tools to tap into your true essence inspired her to write poetry over the years.

The poetry, some rhyming some free verse, then inspired her to create books about getting along. In a nutshell, life and growing up is all about having fun and building relationships – a lesson for adults and children both!

Contact PM for energy readings and more information here:
http://patriciaogilvie.com